Glass Engraving
Pattern Book

Glass Engraving Pattern Book

John Everett

Guild of Master Craftsman Publications Ltd

First published 2000 by
Guild of Master Craftsman Publications Ltd
Castle Place, 166 High Street,
Lewes, East Sussex BN7 1XU

ISBN 1 86108 171 5

A catalogue record for this book is available from the
British Library.

Edited by Stephen Haynes
Book and cover design by Fineline Studios

Set in Bembo

Colour origination by Viscan Graphics Pte Ltd (Singapore)
Printed in China by Sun Fung Offset Binding Co Ltd

Contents

Introduction 1

Corner & border designs

Corners for broad picture frame 12

Corners & line border for
narrow picture frame 14

Clip-frame corners 16

Butterfly border 18

Celtic knotwork border 20

Wreaths & cartouches

Oak-leaf & acorn wreath 24

Classical wreath cartouche 26

Classical griffin cartouche 28

Beer-glass crest with motto 30

Ornate ribbon cartouche 32

Three alphabets 34

Abstract & geometrical designs

Abstract string pattern 40

Cloverleaf string pattern 42

Pyramids & Stonehenge 44

Geometrical abstract 46

Chess motif 48

**Wraparound patterns for
glasses & vases**

Abstract mountain scene 52

Flower band 54

Watch faces 56

Molecular model 58

Musical symbols 60

Formal designs

Signs of the zodiac 64

Stylized foliage motif 68

Labours of the months 70

Vine panel 84

Isis & Nephthys 85

Pictorial designs

Arctic tern 90

Fishing fleet 92

River scene 94

Migrating swallows 96

Haymaking 98

About the author 101

Photocopying

The designs in this book have been printed with generous margins so that readers may easily photocopy them to the required size for their own private use; but please note that they may not be reproduced commercially without the permission of the designer and copyright owner.

Acknowledgement

I would like to thank Fredrik Jacobson and the team at Minicraft for their kind assistance in providing technical details of engraving equipment.

Introduction

The art of engraving various forms of glass is not new; in fact, it is many centuries old. What is new, however, is the easy availability of modern tools and equipment, including diamond engraving points, which not only make the whole process much more enjoyable and easy to do, but bring the art of glass engraving within the reach of everyone who wishes to try it.

Engraving is, in effect, simply scratching the surface of the glass in order to create a pattern or picture which produces an attractive effect when the light strikes it. This 'scratching', or rather engraving, can be varied in terms of both the width and the depth of the engraved line, and it is this variation, together with the use of hatching – small, closely spaced parallel lines within an area of the design – which creates the play of light on the surface of the glass and forms the essence of any engraved design.

Most forms of glass found in the home can be successfully engraved with a vast array of patterns, pictures and the like. **The exception is toughened or 'safety' glass, which is made as the windscreens of motor vehicles used to be, and would almost certainly shatter if engraving were to be attempted on it.** The more normal types of glass, such as are commonly used in the manufacture of drinking glasses, flower vases, glazed furniture, picture frames and mirrors, can be readily engraved in any way you like.

Safety

It is worth pointing out a few things before you begin engraving, so you can enjoy your work with as little trouble as possible. The first, and probably the most obvious, consideration is to be comfortable. This includes having adequate lighting so you can engrave accurately and without eyestrain. Take a little time to decide where you will carry out your engraving. It may be sitting at a kitchen table, or in a workshop if you have one. Make sure you have a suitable work light to hand and that the ambient temperature is comfortable for fine detail work. You cannot engrave well if you are cold, as it is your hands that will suffer first and you will not be able to control your engraver well.

The next thing to consider is the fact that engraving on glass will produce fine glass dust. Have a cloth on hand to wipe away this dust from your workpiece as you proceed, and make sure it is contained safely. A plastic refuse sack is useful for containing the

Using a piece of soft cloth to clear away glass dust resulting from the engraving process. Packs of ordinary household dusters can be purchased quite cheaply and are ideal for this particular operation

residue of your engraving. Take great care not to inhale this dust; if you want to peer closely at the engraved lines as you work, then you really must use a dust mask. These are available at any tool store for very little cost, and the slight inconvenience of wearing one is far preferable to the problems which can ensue from inhaling glass dust. Safety goggles are also advisable; these can be bought from any do-it-yourself store, and can be worn over spectacles.

In selecting the glass you wish to engrave, make absolutely sure it is not manufactured from any form of 'safety' or heatproof glass. This type of glass usually has a logo etched into its surface indicating that it is heatproof, shatterproof or similar; if in doubt, consult the manufacturer.

A selection of glasses, mirrors and vases ready for engraving. These can all be bought quite cheaply at local bargain stores or jumble sales. Most plain glass is fine for engraving, with the exception of 'shatterproof' or safety glass (including Pyrex and similar heatproof types), which are liable to shatter

The cheaper forms of drinking glass, available from most bargain stores in sets of three or four, are great to practice with; it won't cost you much to try out ideas on these before committing yourself to a more expensive type of glass for your actual engraving.

Most picture frames have glass which is easily engraved, as do many types of furniture intended for the living area of your home, and these can be embellished with engravings to enhance their overall effect within your own room decor. Mirrors can also be successfully engraved. The designs used here should not, of course, prevent the mirror fulfilling its original purpose – unless you intend the mirror merely for light reflection, in which case an overall design can be applied to good effect.

When you finish an engraving session, make sure you wipe down your surfaces with a damp cloth and dispose of it safely in your refuse sack. This will ensure that there is no loose glass dust left lying about for anyone to inhale. Glass dust can also damage your workpiece: the silvering on the back of a mirror, for example, could be scratched by the fine dust.

A final point worth mentioning, and this applies to all engraved items, is that they can no longer be considered 'dishwasher safe'. The high temperatures encountered within the cycle of a dishwasher could well result in your carefully engraved masterpiece becoming a handful of broken pieces. Bear in mind that glass is cut to size by scoring it so as to weaken it along the line where you wish it to break, and that is pretty much

what engraving does to the whole surface. There is an inherent weakness left after engraving has been completed, which could well make the glass succumb to the heat of the dishwasher water. For safety, wash engraved items in warm soapy water by hand only.

Engraving tools

If you don't already have an engraving tool, it is worth considering carefully what type will suit you best. The three basic types which are generally available are illustrated below. Try, if you can, to handle each type at your local hobby or craft store; test the weight and feel of each type and find the one which seems most comfortable.

Bear in mind the length of time you expect to spend engraving at each session. If you want to engrave only for short periods and not too often, then the **vibratory engraver** may well be for

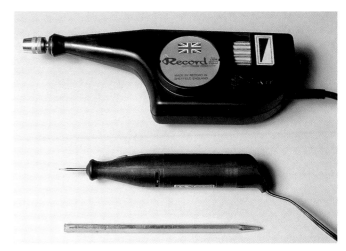

The three main types of engraving tool generally available. From top to bottom: vibratory engraver, rotary engraver, hand engraver

you. This looks somewhat like a pistol drill, and the movement of the point can be adjusted by a knob on the side of the tool. For engraving, the vibratory movement is set at its minimum to avoid breaking the glass. Longer strokes can be used for woodcarving and the like; this will make it more versatile as a general-purpose tool than a dedicated engraving pen would be. The basic tool is usually supplied with a range of bits to permit engraving at various widths and depths. Because the tip does not rotate, this type of engraver is less likely to slip off a rounded surface such as a glass or vase; but it is much heavier than the rotary type of machine and is tiring to use for long periods.

If you want the tool only for engraving, then a purpose-made engraving pen may well be the answer.

The commonest type is the **rotary engraver**, which consists of a high-speed, low-voltage motor and a simple chuck into which the engraver bits are inserted. The unit is normally run from a mains supply via its built-in voltage adapter. This type of tool is light in weight and simple to use. It is held like a pen, and a push-button is located near the chuck, in the place where the forefinger naturally falls; the tool runs only when light pressure is applied to the button. The engraving point rotates at high speed so that only a light touch is required to make an engraved line on the glass. This type of pen normally uses diamond engraving points, which are not as expensive as you might imagine, since they are made from small diamond chips which are in effect waste material. The pen is usually

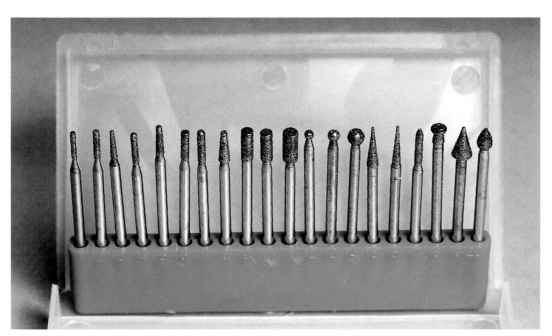

This typical set of diamond engraving points includes several which are more suited to internal grinding applications and the like, but is still a worthwhile addition to the ones already supplied with the engraving pen

supplied with a small selection of these points in different widths, and further sets can be bought quite cheaply from many hobby and craft suppliers.

The final type is the **hand engraver**. This is simply a metal 'pen' with an engraving point permanently fitted in the end, where a pen nib would normally be. This tip can be either tungsten carbide or diamond. Tungsten-carbide points can be readily sharpened with a small diamond honing stone, obtainable from most tool suppliers; it is surprising how quickly the point can be become blunted when engraving glass. This tool is great for straight lines, as used in the 'string pattern' type of design (see pages 40–3), since you can use it with a ruler in much the same way as you would rule a straight line with a pencil. It is, of course, much slower and more laborious than the mechanized types, but it has its place within the range of engraving possibilities.

Engraving on picture-frame glass

There are a few safety points to consider when adding engraved detail to the glass of a picture frame. Firstly, the edges of the sheet of glass are very often rough, and consequently can be sharp. This roughness can easily be removed by rubbing along the edges of the glass with a whetstone (a diamond one is best), carefully rounding over the edges to leave them safely smooth. Check the finish by looking at it rather than running your finger along it, as any remaining roughness could take a slice from your finger.

Another precaution worth mentioning is to support the glass on a thin sheet of foam rubber (latex foam) or polystyrene – or even a towel – which will act as a shock absorber to prevent the glass fracturing as you

The sheet of glass has been securely taped down over the engraving pattern to prevent any movement of the glass or pattern during engraving; it is best to lay a sheet of thin foam down on the table or bench first

engrave, particularly if you get a little carried away with your engraving and push down a bit too hard. A thin sheet of foam is probably best, as it will usually have a smoother surface than a fluffy towel, and will therefore provide firmer support.

Finally, ensure that your glass is securely fixed down before you begin work. Lay your engraving pattern down on the sheet of foam (or whatever you are using) and tape it in place with a few pieces of masking tape; then lay your sheet of glass on top so that the pattern shows through in the right position, and tape the glass down onto your foam sheet so that it cannot move around and spoil the engraving. If you are using the vibratory type of engraver, the foam layer also acts as a

shock absorber, reducing the risk of fracturing the glass by excess pressure on the engraving tool.

Engraving on glasses and vases

These will generally be round or roughly round in shape, so it is well worth taking a little time to make up a supporting cradle such as the one illustrated below. This will protect the glass as well as keeping it still while you are engraving. Additionally, it will enable you to look straight down through the thickness of the glass at the engraving pattern inside, so you will avoid the parallax error caused by refraction within the thickness of the

When engraving glasses and small vases, it is helpful to make up a rest for the glass so that it can be held at a convenient angle for security and accuracy

glass itself. If you look through the wall of the glass at an angle with an engraving pattern in place behind it, you will notice by just how much the apparent image of the pattern moves around as you alter your viewing angle; by rotating the glass in its cradle as you work, you can ensure that you are always looking vertically down at it.

The example shown consists of a pair of shaped supports made from scraps of softwood. The inner surface of each piece is cut to form part of a circle, roughly corresponding to the shape of the glass to be engraved. They are mounted on a base to hold them together, and foam rubber glued to the upper surfaces provides adequate protection for the glass. The resilience of the foam allows the cradle to accommodate a range of glass sizes.

You may sometimes prefer to engrave with the glass on your knee or in some other position, rather than secured in a cradle. It is useful in this case to cut a support piece from thin foam rubber which can be wrapped round the glass, particularly if the glass is straight-sided. The piece of foam will not only protect the glass, but will also provide a safety barrier between the glass and yourself should the glass be accidentally broken. A piece of foam can also be used inside a straight-sided glass to hold the engraving pattern in place without the need for adhesive tape.

The hand rest shown here is also useful to support your wrist as you engrave. Without a support, even a fairly short engraving session will leave your arm and shoulders tired and tense. This simple device allows the engraver to be used for lengthy periods without undue strain on either the hand or the

Cutting a supporting piece from thin foam rubber (latex foam) to wrap round a straight-sided glass

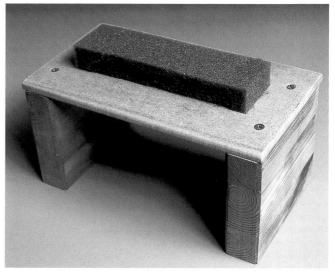

An arm or hand rest for use in conjunction with the glass cradle

wrist. Again, it is simply made up from scraps of softwood or MDF, with a foam-rubber pad on which to rest the hand while engraving. The overall width and height of the hand rest should be sufficient to clear the glass being engraved; otherwise, the dimensions are not critical.

The photograph opposite shows the glass cradle and hand rest in use.

Before making up your engraving pattern from the designs given in the book, it is helpful to know the precise circumference of the glass to be engraved. This can easily be checked with a tape measure, allowing an accurate enlargement to be made on a photocopy machine.

Engraving on mirrors

With mirrors, of course, it is not possible to lay the pattern underneath the glass and follow it with your engraving pen. The easiest solution is to apply a thin, smooth coat of water-based white paint to the surface of the

Engraving in progress, showing the correct positions for the glass cradle and hand rest

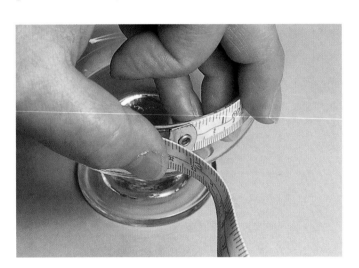

Measuring the circumference of the glass with a tape measure will enable you to enlarge the pattern to the correct size on a photocopier

Using carbon paper to trace the design onto a mirror which has been coated with water-based white paint

mirror. Poster paint and acrylic are both suitable. You can now trace the outlines of your engraving pattern directly onto the white paint via a sheet of carbon paper. If you are doing an intricate design, trace only the main outlines and other important features and engrave these first. You can add the remaining detail later, once you have the main outlines in place. In most cases, once the main features and outlines are in position, no further tracing will be needed: the detail can be completed by eye, with reference to the individual outlines already engraved. You can engrave straight through the paint into the glass surface. Once you have finished your engraving, simply wash off the residue of the white paint to reveal the completed design.

Hatching

Hatching produces a visual effect which can vary between light and dark, depending on the spacing of the lines. A picture on the page of a book is broken up into dots, with a higher 'dot density' giving a stronger tone, and much the same effect can be achieved in drawing or engraving by a pattern of either dots or short lines. There are no set rules for hatching: the visual effect of the engraving is what matters. It therefore follows that whatever form of hatching is used should suit the individual situation. If the area to be filled is round, then hatching lines following the circular shape could well be suitable, whereas for a rock or a mountain, a more informal hatching following the strata of the rocks might be more effective. The Haymaking pattern on pages 98–9 is a particularly good introduction to the various kinds of hatching.

Hatching lines can be made lighter and more delicate by using a smaller engraving tip, or bolder by changing to a larger point. The choice will depend largely on the subject matter and also on your own preferences. For a design which requires a bold effect you might choose a larger point; for other subjects and treatments a much lighter, more ethereal effect might well be your choice, in which case a much smaller point, used with a lighter touch, would be more appropriate. Short lines, longer lines, dots, small circles – in fact any shape that suits the design being worked – are all appropriate as long as they produce the desired visual effect.

If you have no previous experience of engraving, it is a good idea to try out a pattern or two on a sheet of glass from an old photograph frame before buying new items to work on. Get the feel of the engraving tool you have until you are reasonably comfortable with its operation. Practise changing over from one point size to another, and get an idea of the effect each engraving point produces. Then you can try out your first design for real. With a little practice, you will quickly improve your technique and the quality of your engraving; after all, in engraving as in so much else, only practice makes perfect.

Corner &
border designs

All the designs in this section are confined
to the edges of a rectangular piece of glass,
which makes them ideal for use on mirrors,
picture frames, or any other situation where
the main part of the glass panel needs to
be left clear

Corners for broad picture frame

These decorative corner motifs can be added to an existing picture frame to complement the picture inside. The picture is first removed from the frame, and the limits of the frame are marked on the glass with a water-soluble marker pen (see the photograph below) so that the pattern can be laid symmetrically in all four corners of the glass. The glass can now be turned over and laid in position on the engraving pattern in the certain knowledge that all four corners will line up correctly when the frame is reassembled with its picture in place.

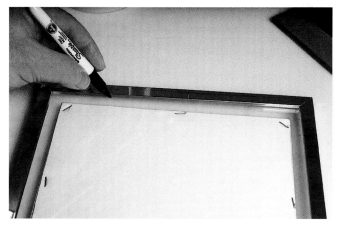

Corners
& line border

for narrow picture frame

This pattern is for a decorative border which could be used equally well on a mirror, a furniture glazing panel or a picture frame; the photograph shows it applied to a picture frame. Picture 1 shows the panel of glass being centred over the engraving pattern. The glass is then taped down securely in position so that it cannot move in relation to the pattern during the engraving process. Picture 2 shows the straight-line part of the design being engraved with the assistance of a straight-edged piece of wood to ensure that the lines really are straight in the completed project.

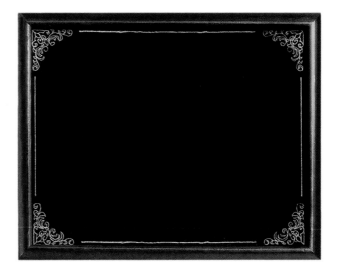

2

1

Clip-frame corners

This pattern provides a set of decorative engraved corners for a clip frame, such as might well be used to display a certificate. This treatment adds a little ornament to an otherwise plain and uninteresting frame.

If your frame is not the same size as the drawing, you can adjust the design as shown in the small photograph. Lay the glass over one corner of the design, then draw round it so as to make a reference mark on the paper pattern. Each corner of the glass in turn can then be aligned with this mark and engraved from the pattern.

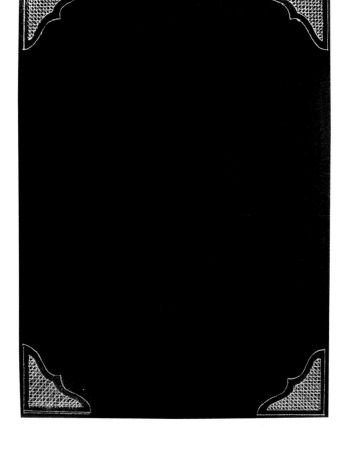

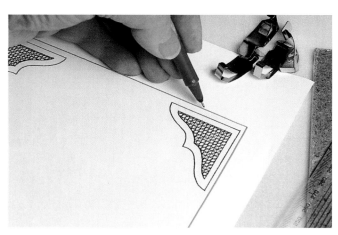

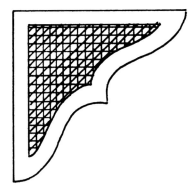
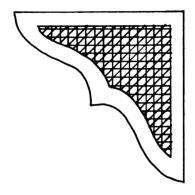
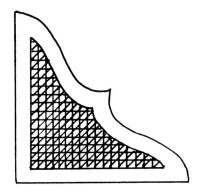
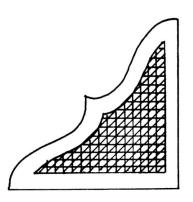

Butterfly border

This design of butterflies joined together in a straight-line border is suitable for a picture frame, a mirror or even a furniture panel. In this instance the design is applied to a picture frame, and is intended to be seen against the picture mount or overlay used within the frame. A rule or straightedge should be used to ensure that the straight lines in the pattern remain straight in the engraving.

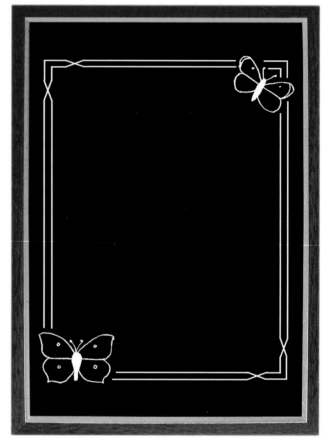

Celtic knotwork border

The small photographs show two alternative ways of treating the finished engraving. In Picture 1, black acrylic paint is being rubbed into the engraved lines to produce an etched effect. Picture 2 shows the frame finished with a gold metallic paste, which is obtainable from craft and hobby outlets. You can, of course, use any colour you wish, or leave the design in its natural colour as shown in the main photograph. Any of the designs in this book can be embellished further by the addition of colouring material if desired.

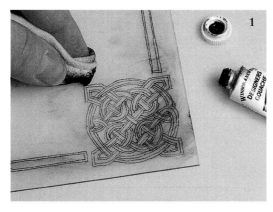

Wreaths &
cartouches

A cartouche is an ornamental frame or
border, often with a motif or inscription in the
centre. Any of the designs in this section could
have lettering added if desired

Oak-leaf & acorn wreath

This oak-leaf and acorn design is intended to echo and reinforce the pattern on the frame of the mirror, which was made on the scrollsaw. The mirror is first given a coat of white poster paint so that the pattern can be readily transferred to the surface using a sheet of carbon paper. In order to centre the pattern correctly on the mirror's surface, the carbon paper and the engraving pattern should be cut to the correct size before applying them to the mirror. The pattern can now be engraved directly through the coat of poster paint and into the glass itself.

Classical wreath cartouche

with initials

This decorative cartouche has space in the centre for initials to 'personalize' the glass. A selection of sample alphabets has been provided on pages 35–7 for use with this and other designs in this section, but many alternative styles are available from the average computer or word processor.

First make a full-sized copy of the border design, and then locate your initial letters within the border, arranging them so that they form a balanced design. (As the small photograph shows, I experimented with two different layouts for the letters.) Then trace the letters onto the pattern and cut it out with as little surrounding blank paper as possible;

the thinner the paper, the easier it will be to form it accurately to the shape of the glass. The pattern is then taped inside the glass (as in the small photograph), which can be filled with cloth as an added insurance against the tape working loose as you engrave.

Classical griffin cartouche

with initials

This is essentially the same idea as the previous pattern, but the rather 'masculine' design for the border seemed to me to be more suitable for a beer glass. The procedure is precisely the same as for the previous pattern; the small photograph shows the initials being chosen for correct size and balance within the frame of the engraved border.

Beer-glass crest
with motto

This design is intended for a beer tankard; the Latin inscription NUNC EST BIBENDUM translates as 'Time for a drink'. The engraved inscription is arranged to be on the opposite side of the tankard to the handle. In this way it will be visible while the glass is in use, and the engraving will not cause any discomfort by intruding into the parts of the glass where the mouth will be applied, regardless of whether the user is left- or right-handed. The small photograph shows the pattern being taped inside the glass, as before; this is much easier to do on a straight-sided glass than on any other type.

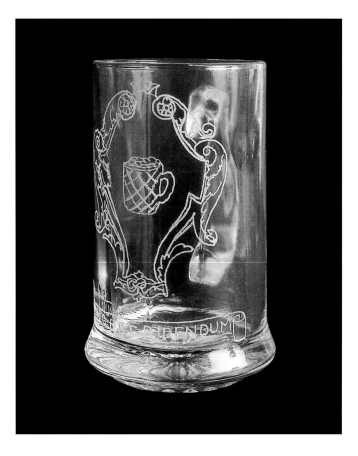

NUNC EST BIBENDUM

Ornate ribbon cartouche

This large border or frame is another pattern suitable for a furniture glazing panel; this time it is important that the outer borders should be central within the glass panel, and the small photograph shows this being checked.

WREATHS & CARTOUCHES

Three alphabets

T he alphabets on these pages can be used for adding lettering to any of the cartouche designs.

A B C

A B C

a b c d e

A B C D E

F G H I J

K L M N O

P Q R S T

U V W X Y

Z

Cursive capitals

A B C D
E F G H I
J K L M N
O P Q R
S T U V
W X Y Z

Italic capitals

Celtic alphabet

abcddefghi
klmnopqrs
tuvuxyz

Abstract & geometrical designs

These designs take their inspiration from a range of sources,
from string pictures to 1930s Art Deco. Most of these cover a
greater part of the glass surface than the preceding patterns,
but still allow the glass to be seen through

Abstract string pattern

This redesign of a 'string and pin' pattern much favoured in the 1960s is shown applied to a sheet of glass fitted to a room divider. The pattern is first taped down securely on a foam backing sheet, and the glass is then taped in position around its edges. As this design consists purely of straight lines, a straightedge as a guide for the engraving tool is an absolute must. The engraving pen is first fitted with a large engraving point and the bolder border lines are engraved. This helps to give a reference frame for the complete design. Next, the dividing lines of the pattern are put in place with a finer point so that the remainder of the pattern can be engraved accurately.

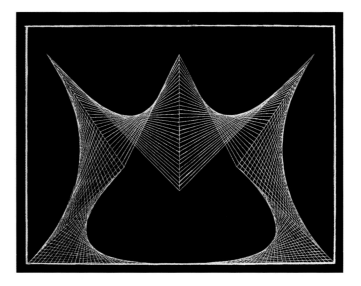

The straightedge shown here is a steel rule taped on top of a long plastic ruler. The steel gives a hard edge for the *shaft* of the engraving point to run against, while the plastic provides a gap between the edge of the steel rule and the work surface to ensure that only the shaft of the engraving point is in contact with the edge of the steel rule – otherwise the actual engraving point, with its coating of diamonds, would very quickly spoil the straightedge.

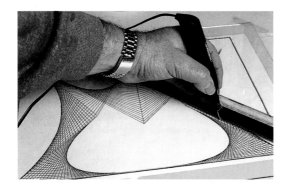

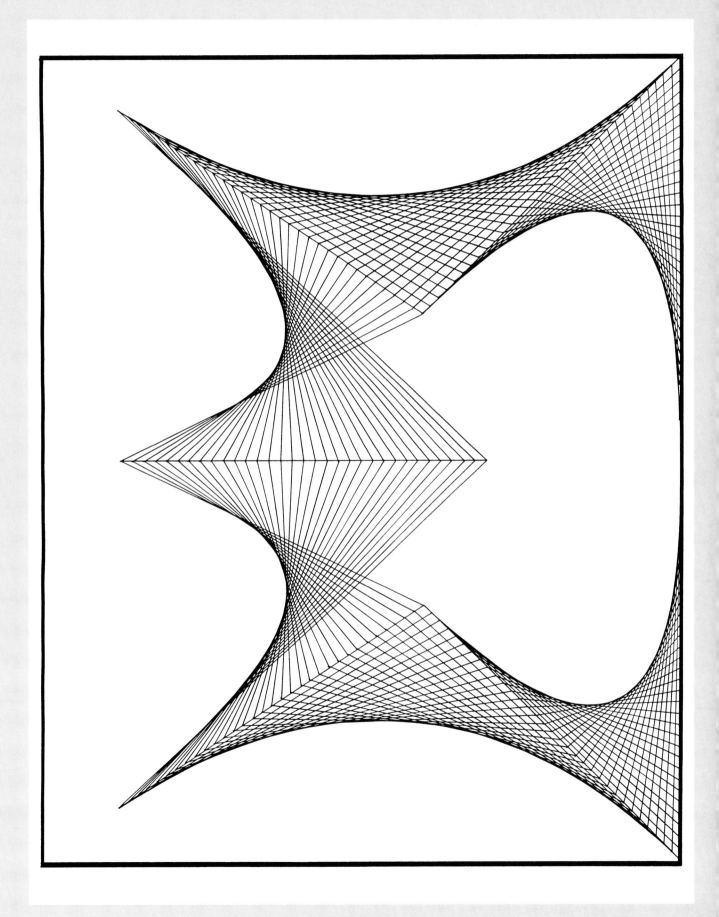

Cloverleaf string pattern

T his smaller 'string and pin' pattern has been designed for use with a mirror, and leaves the centre portion of the reflecting surface clear. The mirror is first coated with white water-based paint; then, as shown in the photograph below, the engraving pattern and carbon paper are cut to fit the precise dimensions of the mirror, since accurate placing of the pattern is crucial to avoid a lopsided appearance. The main lines are engraved first and then the interconnecting lines are added section by section until the design is complete. The final step is to wash off the residue of the white paint.

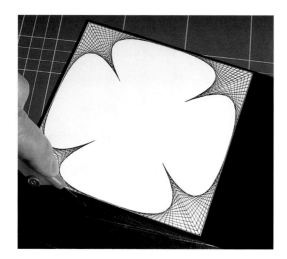

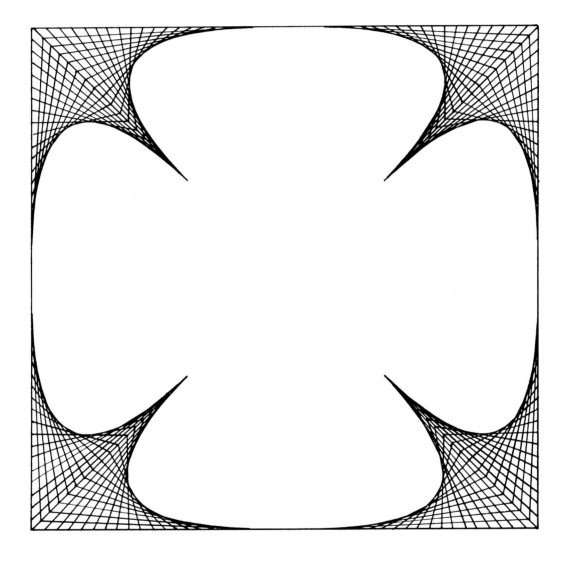

Pyramids & Stonehenge

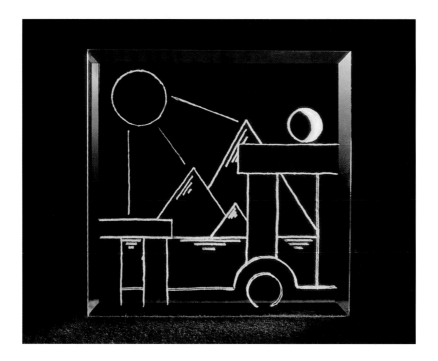

T his bold abstract design with an Art Deco flavour is ideal for a small mirror which is used chiefly for its light-reflecting properties, rather than for producing an optically perfect reflection. The pattern contains both straight lines and circles; a straightedge is again essential, and a circle template (seen on the far right in the small photograph) can be used to form the circles accurately. A piece of thick card placed underneath the template will prevent it being chewed up by the engraving point.

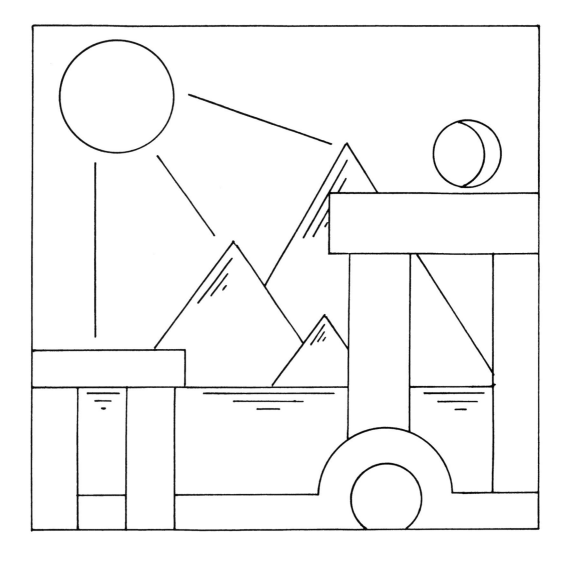

Geometrical abstract

A purely abstract design suitable for decorating a furniture glazing panel. Begin by drawing the diagonals on the sheet of glass, as shown below, to locate the centre. Use a water-based marker pen for this, so the marks can be cleaned off easily after the engraving pattern has been accurately positioned. The lozenge shape in the centre of the pattern can be located easily. With the pattern taped in position on the engraving mat, the glass sheet can be carefully aligned and then taped securely in place for engraving. A straightedge is recommended to ensure accuracy.

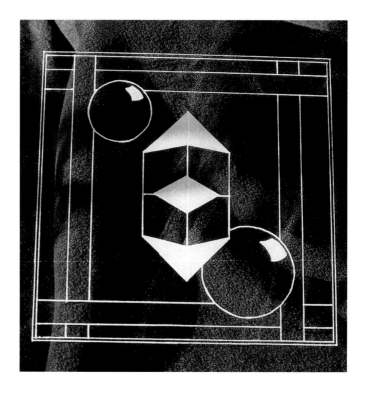

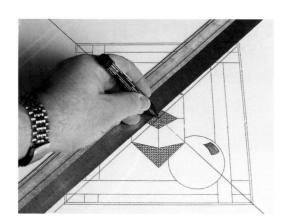

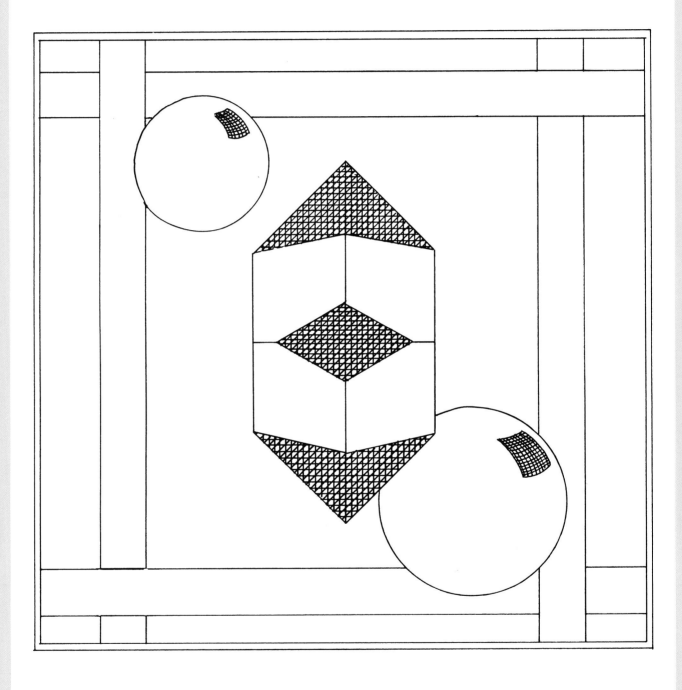

Chess motif

The final design in this section is also for a furniture glazing panel. The hatching lines in the pattern can be engraved using a straightedge for accuracy, or you can simply engrave the whole of the hatched area to give a frosted-glass effect. Centre the design within the glass sheet for best results.

Wraparound patterns for glasses & vases

The patterns in this section are designed to go all the way round a curved surface, which makes them ideal for straight-sided glasses or vases without handles, though they could easily be adapted for many other uses as well

Abstract mountain scene

This pattern is a complete wraparound design for a wine glass. First use a tape measure to find the circumference of the glass you intend to use; the pattern can then be adjusted accordingly, enlarging or reducing on a photocopier if necessary. Make sure the top of the design comes a little way down the glass so that there is no roughness to be felt near the rim.

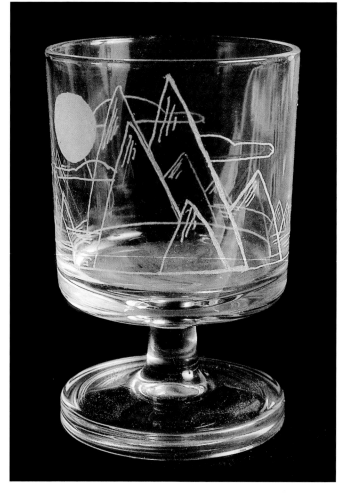

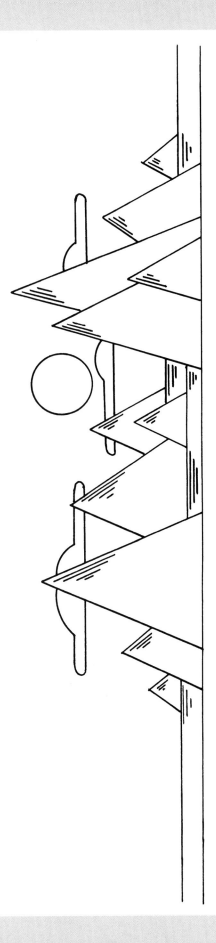

Flower band

This wraparound design is suitable for a shallow sundae glass. The lower photograph shows the photocopied pattern being trimmed so that the design will be centred within the height of the glass. In this way, when the pattern is taped in position inside the glass, the top of the paper can be aligned with the rim of the glass to ensure that the ends of the pattern will meet accurately.

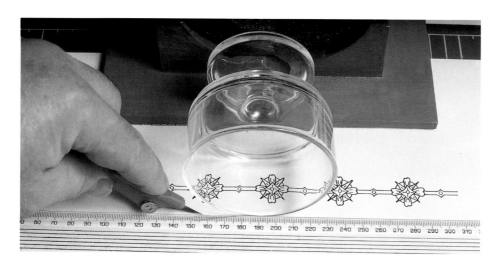

Watch faces

The technique for this pattern is the same as for the previous one. The watch faces all show different times of day which are suitable for eating desserts!

Molecular model

Adecorative wraparound design for a taller glass. The engraving pattern is first placed within the glass and temporarily taped together so that the design covers the whole circumference of the glass. (The small photograph shows the position of the join being marked on the paper.) You can then take the pattern out and customize the design to suit your particular glass by connecting up the molecules across the join in the paper. Once you have drawn all the elements of the design together in this way, reinsert the completed pattern into the glass and carry out the engraving as usual.

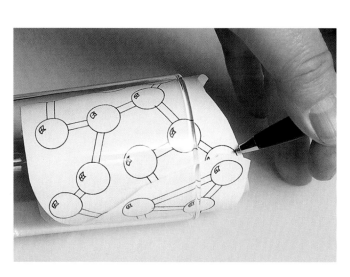

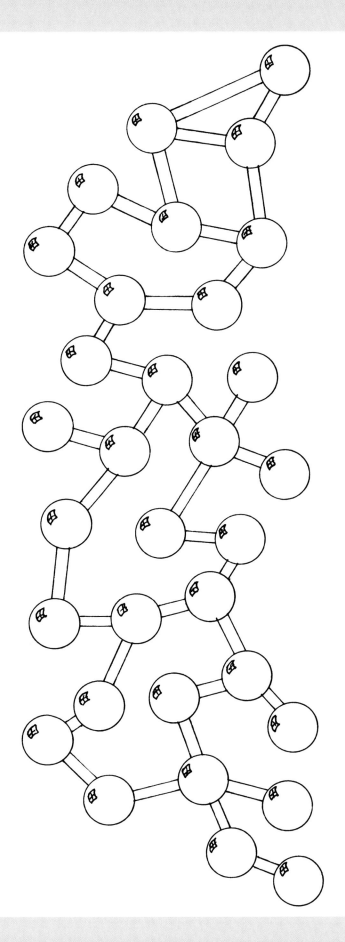

Musical symbols

T his pattern is identical in its execution to the previous one, but this time random musical notation and keyboard elements have been used as the basic design.

Formal designs

These classical and traditional motifs are suitable for a wide
variety of applications. They include two complete
sequences of calendar-related designs which could either be
engraved as a set or used to personalize an item to suit the
owner's birth date

Signs of the zodiac

These patterns for all the individual star signs work well on mirrors and picture frames, as well as on the drinking glass shown here. For use on a drinking glass, the pattern is first cut to size with as little margin around it as possible. This makes it easier to stick in place inside the glass without any wrinkles forming (which can be a problem, especially if the bowl of the glass has compound curves). The glass can then be filled with a scrap of soft material or polystyrene chips, which will help to press the pattern up against the side of the glass so it does not move around while you are handling it.

In the background of the small photograph you will see the glass rest described in the Introduction. Using this in conjunction with the hand rest will make it feasible to engrave a whole set of these glasses in a single session.

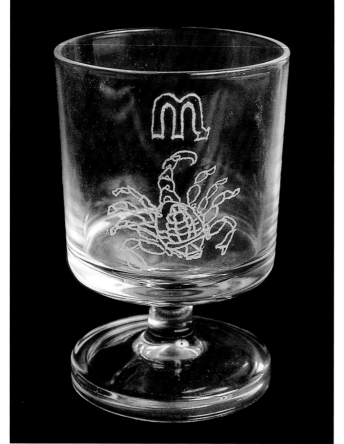

Aries
21 March–20 April

Taurus
21 April–21 May

Gemini
22 May–21 Jun

Cancer
22 June–22 July

Leo
23 July–23 August

Virgo
24 August–22 September

Libra
23 September–23 October

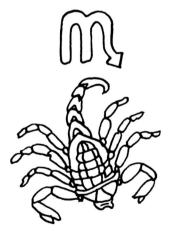

Scorpio
24 October–22 November

Sagittarius
23 November–21 December

Capricorn
22 December–20 January

Aquarius
21 January–18 February

Pisces
19 February–20 March

Stylized foliage motif

This ornate design is suitable as a central embellishment to a furniture glazing panel; alternatively, it could be framed as a picture in its own right, as in Picture 1. This is another instance where the design needs to be centred accurately within the sheet of glass for best effect. Draw in the diagonals of the glass panel with a water-based marker pen, and use this intersection to position your engraving pattern accurately beneath the glass as in Picture 2. In the example shown here, gold paste, available from many hobby and craft outlets, has been rubbed into the completed engraving to enhance the pattern.

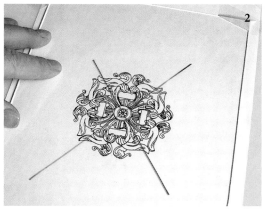

Labours of the months

These twelve patterns are based on medieval woodcuts representing the months of the year and the typical activities associated with them. They are fairly straightforward from an engraving point of view, as the original artist did not use much fine detail. The full set is illustrated here, so that an item of furniture such as a breakfront bookcase could be decorated with a different month on each pane; or specific months could be chosen, perhaps with reference to the owner's birth month. The notes accompanying the patterns explain the illustration for each month.

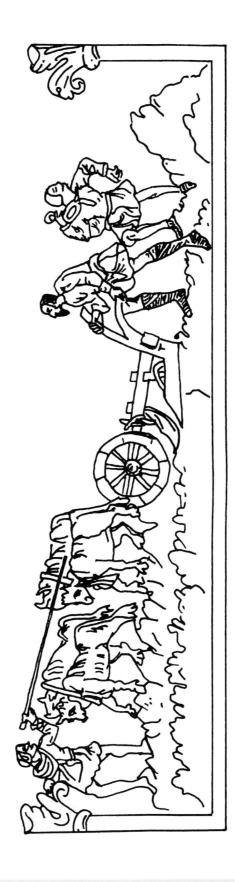

January

The heathen English called this month *Wolf-monath* (*monath* = month), because the wolves were then at their most ravenous. It was also called *Æfter-Yula*, or 'after Yuletide'. Four oxen are drawing a plough; at this time, horses were not used for field labour.

February

The picture shows trees being cut and carted for firewood. The English called February *Sprout-kele*; *kele* means colewort or cabbage, which was extensively used for making broth.

March

This month was dedicated by the English to the goddess Rhoeda and was thus called *Rhede-monath*. It was also known as *Illyd-monath*, or 'stormy month'. The scene shows digging, hoeing and sowing seed. After the introduction of Christianity, March was held in reverence as the month in which Lent began.

April

April was called *Oster-monath*, because the wind generally blew from the east during this month. The scene shows three thegns celebrating a feast by quaffing ale from their drinking horns. On the right is an armed guard with a long spear and on the left are two serving-men. The bench on which the three thegns are seated is adorned with sculptures of formidable-looking animals. The use of chairs or sofas was unknown at this time. The benches placed in the halls were called *mede benc* or *eala benc* – mead or ale benches.

May

This month was called *Trimilki* because the cattle were then milked three times a day.
In the picture, shepherds are watching over their sheep and lambs. May Day was the great
English rural festival.

June

June was sometimes known as *Weyd-monath*, because then the cattle began to 'wade' – that is, feed in the meadows, which at that time were usually marshes. Alternatively, it was called *Midsummer-monath*. This was the time of the year when the English began long sea voyages, and here we see them trimming trees which will be cut down in order to fit out their ships.

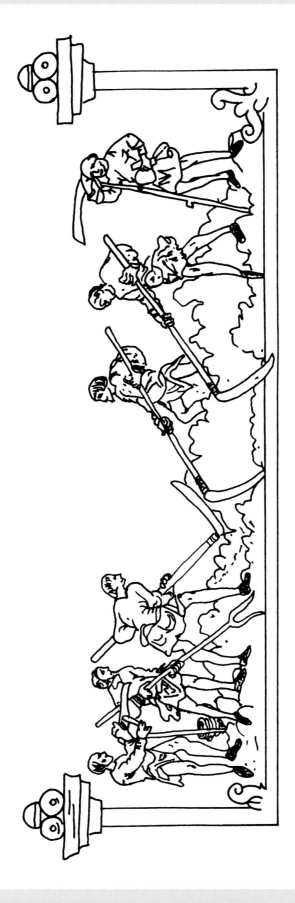

July

This month was called either *Heu-monath* (foliage month) or *Hey-monath* (hay month), this being the month in which they mowed and made hay as shown in the woodcut. It was also called *Lida-aftera*, meaning the second *lida*, or second month after the sun's descent.

August

August was called *Arn-monath* or *Barn-monath*, both meaning 'harvest month'. In the woodcut, the corn is being harvested and loaded onto a cart.

September

This month was called *Gerst-monath* – barley month. It was named from the liquor called *beerlegh* made in that month – the source of our word 'barley'. The woodcut shows a boar hunt in progress.

October

This was *Cold-monath* or *Wyn-monath*: the vine was extensively cultivated in England at that time. The woodcut shows a hawking scene.

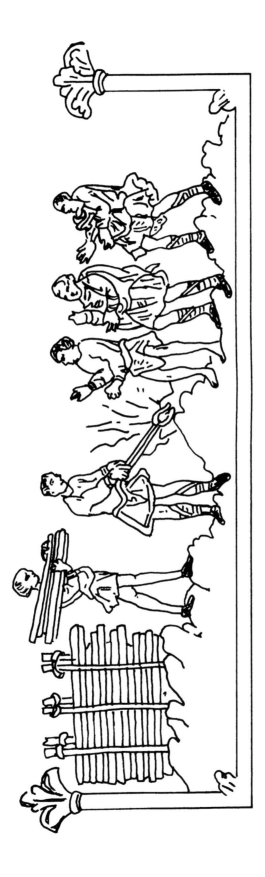

November

This month was known as *Wint-monath* or 'wind month', as this was the season when cold storms began which were generally expected to last until March. It was the custom to light great fires in the open in honour of the gods and to drive away evil spirits. The men in the woodcut are seen at one of these fires.

December

December was called *Ærra Geola* because the sun then 'turns his glorious course'. After the introduction of Christianity, it was called *Heilig-monath* or 'holy month'. December was, above all, a month of festivity. Before the introduction of Christianity, Christmas was the feast of Thor and the wassail bowl circulated as briskly in honour of the heathen god as it has since done at the Christian festival. The figures in the woodcut are winnowing and threshing corn.

Vine panel

This pattern is for a large, plain glass flower vase, and adds a little interest to the lower part of the flower arrangement which would otherwise feature only stems. Once the engraving pattern has been taped in position, the whole vase can be filled with polystyrene chips, as shown, to keep the pattern flat against the glass and prevent it slipping.

Isis & Nephthys

Two ancient Egyptian goddesses, Isis and her sister Nephthys, are placed one either side of a rectangular mirror. This gives an interesting effect when you look in the mirror to find your own face placed centrally between the two decorative characters. As with all small mirrors, the original cutting pattern and carbon paper are cut to exactly the right size before transferring the pattern onto the painted surface, in order to ensure a good balance of the finished subject (Picture 1). Picture 2 shows the engraving under way, beginning with the main outlines of the figures which will be filled in later. Note that there is no need to apply paint to the centre portion of the mirror, where no engraving will be done.

1

2

Pictorial designs

The patterns in this final section are pictures to be enjoyed in their own right, rather than simply embellishments to functional objects. They may look daunting at first, but a methodical approach, defining main outlines first and filling in details afterwards, is all that is needed to engrave them successfully

Arctic tern

This pattern of an arctic tern in flight makes an ideal decoration for the glazed panel of a lounge unit. In the lower photograph, the bill and feet of the tern – which are in reality a bright orange-red colour – are being picked out with glass paint as an added decoration. This is the only part of the real bird which has any colour, and so makes for a realistic representation.

Fishing fleet

This scene of a fishing fleet in action is suitable for a mirror which is used merely as a light reflector and not as an optical mirror. The pattern and carbon paper are cut to the shape of the mirror before transferring the design, so that the pattern can be accurately located on the mirror.

River scene

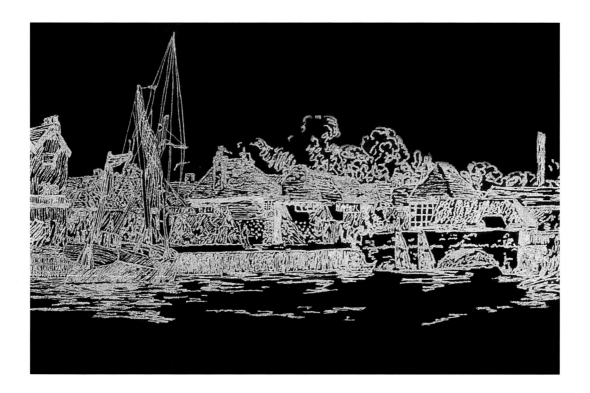

This riverside scene with boats and bridge is an ideal one to adorn a furniture panel. The engraving is quite straightforward. Place your sheet of glass accurately over the pattern so that the picture will appear exactly where you want it to be. Then engrave the main outlines of the various picture elements and finally add the shading and hatching lines to complete the scene. A magnifying glass on a stand may help with the fine detail.

Migrating swallows

This pattern is of migrating swallows forming up over rocks in the sea ready for their onward flight to warmer climates. The pattern has been applied to a fairly large mirror in this example, but will work equally well on a furniture glazing panel. As usual, a coat of white poster paint has been applied to the mirror surface to allow the pattern to be transferred via a sheet of carbon paper. The small photograph shows the carbon paper being cut exactly to size so that the pattern can be accurately located on the mirror.

Haymaking

Although this haymaking scene with its ox-cart and figures seems complicated, it is actually quite easy to engrave. The important thing is to engrave the main outlines of the various elements first; you can then finish each element separately. This project will make you thoroughly familiar with the feel of the engraving tool, as there are many different types of outline and hatching to be completed within the picture. Since the design fills the entire pane of glass, this pattern is ideally suited to a furniture panel rather than a mirror or picture frame. This intricate design will require frequent

application of your duster to remove the glass dust and, in a pattern where there is so much engraving to do, the use of a dust mask is even more advisable than usual.

About the author

John Everett is a technical artist and photographer with a long-standing interest in woodwork and other crafts. He lives and works in Wales, where he produces craft kits and projects for a range of individuals and organizations, including schools and colleges.

As well as being a regular contributor to craft magazines, he is the author of three other books published by GMC Publications: *The Scrollsaw: Twenty Projects*, *Minidrill: Fifteen Projects* and *Practical Scrollsaw Patterns*.

TITLES AVAILABLE FROM
GMC Publications
BOOKS

CRAFTS

American Patchwork Designs in Needlepoint	Melanie Tacon
A Beginners' Guide to Rubber Stamping	Brenda Hunt
Blackwork: A New Approach	Brenda Day
Celtic Cross Stitch Designs	Carol Phillipson
Celtic Knotwork Designs	Sheila Sturrock
Celtic Knotwork Handbook	Sheila Sturrock
Celtic Spirals and Other Designs	Sheila Sturrock
Collage from Seeds, Leaves and Flowers	Joan Carver
Complete Pyrography	Stephen Poole
Contemporary Smocking	Dorothea Hall
Creating Colour with Dylon	Dylon International
Creative Doughcraft	Patricia Hughes
Creative Embroidery Techniques Using Colour Through Gold	
	Daphne J. Ashby & Jackie Woolsey
The Creative Quilter: Techniques and Projects	Pauline Brown
Decorative Beaded Purses	Enid Taylor
Designing and Making Cards	Glennis Gilruth
Glass Engraving Pattern Book	John Everett
Glass Painting	Emma Sedman
How to Arrange Flowers: A Japanese Approach to English Design	
	Taeko Marvelly
An Introduction to Crewel Embroidery	Mave Glenny
Making and Using Working Drawings for Realistic Model Animals	
	Basil F. Fordham
Making Character Bears	Valerie Tyler
Making Decorative Screens	Amanda Howes
Making Fairies and Fantastical Creatures	Julie Sharp
Making Greetings Cards for Beginners	Pat Sutherland
Making Hand-Sewn Boxes: Techniques and Projects	Jackie Woolsey
Making Knitwear Fit	Pat Ashforth & Steve Plummer
Making Mini Cards, Gift Tags & Invitations	Glennis Gilruth
Making Soft-Bodied Dough Characters	Patricia Hughes
Natural Ideas for Christmas: Fantastic Decorations to Make	
	Josie Cameron-Ashcroft & Carol Cox
Needlepoint: A Foundation Course	Sandra Hardy
Patchwork for Beginners	Pauline Brown
Pyrography Designs	Norma Gregory
Pyrography Handbook (Practical Crafts)	Stephen Poole
Ribbons and Roses	Lee Lockheed
Rose Windows for Quilters	Angela Besley
Rubber Stamping with Other Crafts	Lynne Garner
Sponge Painting	Ann Rooney
Tassel Making for Beginners	Enid Taylor
Tatting Collage	Lindsay Rogers
Temari: A Traditional Japanese Embroidery Technique	Margaret Ludlow
Theatre Models in Paper and Card	Robert Burgess
Wool Embroidery and Design	Lee Lockheed

WOODWORKING

Bird Boxes and Feeders for the Garden	Dave Mackenzie
Complete Woodfinishing	Ian Hosker
David Charlesworth's Furniture-Making Techniques	David Charlesworth

Furniture & Cabinetmaking Projects	GMC Publications
Furniture-Making Projects for the Wood Craftsman	GMC Publications
Furniture-Making Techniques for the Wood Craftsman	GMC Publications
Furniture Projects	Rod Wales
Furniture Restoration (Practical Crafts)	Kevin Jan Bonner
Furniture Restoration and Repair for Beginners	Kevin Jan Bonner
Furniture Restoration Workshop	Kevin Jan Bonner
Green Woodwork	Mike Abbott
Kevin Ley's Furniture Projects	Kevin Ley
Making & Modifying Woodworking Tools	Jim Kingshott
Making Chairs and Tables	GMC Publications
Making Classic English Furniture	Paul Richardson
Making Little Boxes from Wood	John Bennett
Making Shaker Furniture	Barry Jackson
Making Woodwork Aids and Devices	Robert Wearing
Minidrill: Fifteen Projects	John Everett
Pine Furniture Projects for the Home	Dave Mackenzie
Practical Scrollsaw Patterns	John Everett
Router Magic: Jigs, Fixtures and Tricks to	
Unleash your Router's Full Potential	Bill Hylton
Routing for Beginners	Anthony Bailey
Scrollsaw Projects	GMC Publications
The Scrollsaw: Twenty Projects	John Everett
Sharpening: The Complete Guide	Jim Kingshott
Sharpening Pocket Reference Book	Jim Kingshott
Space-Saving Furniture Projects	Dave Mackenzie
Stickmaking: A Complete Course	Andrew Jones & Clive George
Stickmaking Handbook	Andrew Jones & Clive George
Test Reports: The Router and Furniture & Cabinetmaking	GMC Publications
Veneering: A Complete Course	Ian Hosker
Woodfinishing Handbook (Practical Crafts)	Ian Hosker
Woodworking with the Router: Professional	
Router Techniques any Woodworker can Use	Bill Hylton & Fred Matlack
The Workshop	Jim Kingshott

WOODCARVING

The Art of the Woodcarver	GMC Publications
Carving Architectural Detail in Wood: The Classical Tradition	Frederick Wilbur
Carving Birds & Beasts	GMC Publications
Carving Nature: Wildlife Studies in Wood	Frank Fox-Wilson
Carving Realistic Birds	David Tippey
Decorative Woodcarving	Jeremy Williams
Elements of Woodcarving	Chris Pye
Essential Tips for Woodcarvers	GMC Publications
Essential Woodcarving Techniques	Dick Onians
Further Useful Tips for Woodcarvers	GMC Publications
Lettercarving in Wood: A Practical Course	Chris Pye
Making & Using Working Drawings for Realistic Model Animals	
	Basil F. Fordham
Power Tools for Woodcarving	David Tippey
Practical Tips for Turners & Carvers	GMC Publications
Relief Carving in Wood: A Practical Introduction	Chris Pye
Understanding Woodcarving	GMC Publications

Understanding Woodcarving in the Round	*GMC Publications*
Useful Techniques for Woodcarvers	*GMC Publications*
Wildfowl Carving – Volume 1	*Jim Pearce*
Wildfowl Carving – Volume 2	*Jim Pearce*
Woodcarving: A Complete Course	*Ron Butterfield*
Woodcarving: A Foundation Course	*Zoë Gertner*
Woodcarving for Beginners	*GMC Publications*
Woodcarving Tools & Equipment Test Reports	*GMC Publications*
Woodcarving Tools, Materials & Equipment	*Chris Pye*

WOODTURNING

Adventures in Woodturning	*David Springett*
Bert Marsh: Woodturner	*Bert Marsh*
Bowl Turning Techniques Masterclass	*Tony Boase*
Colouring Techniques for Woodturners	*Jan Sanders*
The Craftsman Woodturner	*Peter Child*
Decorative Techniques for Woodturners	*Hilary Bowen*
Fun at the Lathe	*R.C. Bell*
Further Useful Tips for Woodturners	*GMC Publications*
Illustrated Woodturning Techniques	*John Hunnex*
Intermediate Woodturning Projects	*GMC Publications*
Keith Rowley's Woodturning Projects	*Keith Rowley*
Practical Tips for Turners & Carvers	*GMC Publications*
Turning Green Wood	*Michael O'Donnell*
Turning Miniatures in Wood	*John Sainsbury*
Turning Pens and Pencils	*Kip Christensen & Rex Burningham*
Understanding Woodturning	*Ann & Bob Phillips*
Useful Techniques for Woodturners	*GMC Publications*
Useful Woodturning Projects	*GMC Publications*
Woodturning: Bowls, Platters, Hollow Forms, Vases, Vessels, Bottles, Flasks, Tankards, Plates	*GMC Publications*
Woodturning: A Foundation Course (New Edition)	*Keith Rowley*
Woodturning: A Fresh Approach	*Robert Chapman*
Woodturning: An Individual Approach	*Dave Regester*
Woodturning: A Source Book of Shapes	*John Hunnex*
Woodturning Jewellery	*Hilary Bowen*
Woodturning Masterclass	*Tony Boase*
Woodturning Techniques	*GMC Publications*
Woodturning Tools & Equipment Test Reports	*GMC Publications*
Woodturning Wizardry	*David Springett*

UPHOLSTERY

The Upholsterer's Pocket Reference Book	*David James*
Upholstery: A Complete Course (Revised Edition)	*David James*
Upholstery Restoration	*David James*
Upholstery Techniques & Projects	*David James*
Upholstery Tips and Hints	*David James*

TOYMAKING

Designing & Making Wooden Toys	*Terry Kelly*
Fun to Make Wooden Toys & Games	*Jeff & Jennie Loader*
Restoring Rocking Horses	*Clive Green & Anthony Dew*
Scrollsaw Toy Projects	*Ivor Carlyle*
Scrollsaw Toys for All Ages	*Ivor Carlyle*
Wooden Toy Projects	*GMC Publications*

DOLLS' HOUSES AND MINIATURES

Architecture for Dolls' Houses	*Joyce Percival*
A Beginners' Guide to the Dolls' House Hobby	*Jean Nisbett*
The Complete Dolls' House Book	*Jean Nisbett*
The Dolls' House 1/24 Scale: A Complete Introduction	*Jean Nisbett*
Dolls' House Accessories, Fixtures and Fittings	*Andrea Barham*
Dolls' House Bathrooms: Lots of Little Loos	*Patricia King*
Dolls' House Fireplaces and Stoves	*Patricia King*
Easy to Make Dolls' House Accessories	*Andrea Barham*
Heraldic Miniature Knights	*Peter Greenhill*
Make Your Own Dolls' House Furniture	*Maurice Harper*
Making Dolls' House Furniture	*Patricia King*
Making Georgian Dolls' Houses	*Derek Rowbottom*
Making Miniature Gardens	*Freida Gray*
Making Miniature Oriental Rugs & Carpets	*Meik & Ian McNaughton*
Making Period Dolls' House Accessories	*Andrea Barham*
Making 1/12 Scale Character Figures	*James Carrington*
Making Tudor Dolls' Houses	*Derek Rowbottom*
Making Victorian Dolls' House Furniture	*Patricia King*
Miniature Bobbin Lace	*Roz Snowden*
Miniature Embroidery for the Georgian Dolls' House	*Pamela Warner*
Miniature Embroidery for the Victorian Dolls' House	*Pamela Warner*
Miniature Needlepoint Carpets	*Janet Granger*
More Miniature Oriental Rugs & Carpets	*Meik & Ian McNaughton*
Needlepoint 1/12 Scale: Design Collections for the Dolls' House	*Felicity Price*
The Secrets of the Dolls' House Makers	*Jean Nisbett*

GARDENING

Auriculas for Everyone: How to Grow and Show Perfect Plants	*Mary Robinson*
Bird Boxes and Feeders for the Garden	*Dave Mackenzie*
The Birdwatcher's Garden	*Hazel & Pamela Johnson*
Broad-Leaved Evergreens	*Stephen G. Haw*
Companions to Clematis: Growing Clematis with Other Plants	*Marigold Badcock*
Creating Contrast with Dark Plants	*Freya Martin*
Gardening with Wild Plants	*Julian Slatcher*
Hardy Perennials: A Beginner's Guide	*Eric Sawford*
The Living Tropical Greenhouse: Creating a Haven for Butterflies	*John & Maureen Tampion*
Orchids are Easy: A Beginner's Guide to their Care and Cultivation	*Tom Gilland*
Plants that Span the Seasons	*Roger Wilson*

VIDEOS

Drop-in and Pinstuffed Seats	*David James*
Stuffover Upholstery	*David James*
Elliptical Turning	*David Springett*
Woodturning Wizardry	*David Springett*
Turning Between Centres: The Basics	*Dennis White*
Turning Bowls	*Dennis White*
Boxes, Goblets and Screw Threads	*Dennis White*
Novelties and Projects	*Dennis White*
Classic Profiles	*Dennis White*
Twists and Advanced Turning	*Dennis White*
Sharpening the Professional Way	*Jim Kingshott*
Sharpening Turning & Carving Tools	*Jim Kingshott*
Bowl Turning	*John Jordan*
Hollow Turning	*John Jordan*
Woodturning: A Foundation Course	*Keith Rowley*
Carving a Figure: The Female Form	*Ray Gonzalez*
The Router: A Beginner's Guide	*Alan Goodsell*
The Scroll Saw: A Beginner's Guide	*John Burke*

MAGAZINES

WOODTURNING ◆ WOODCARVING ◆ FURNITURE & CABINETMAKING
THE ROUTER ◆ WOODWORKING
THE DOLLS' HOUSE MAGAZINE
WATER GARDENING
EXOTIC GARDENING
GARDEN CALENDAR
OUTDOOR PHOTOGRAPHY
BUSINESSMATTERS

The above represents a full list of all titles currently published or scheduled to be published.
All are available direct from the Publishers or through bookshops, newsagents and specialist retailers.
To place an order, or to obtain a complete catalogue, contact:

**GMC Publications,
Castle Place, 166 High Street, Lewes, East Sussex BN7 1XU, United Kingdom
Tel: 01273 488005 Fax: 01273 478606
E-mail: pubs@thegmcgroup.com**

Orders by credit card are accepted

  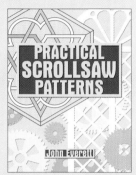